Where Does Everybody Go?

By Dayle Ann Dodds

Illustrated by Pamela Johnson

Houghton Mifflin Company Boston

Atlanta Dallas Geneva, Illinois Palo Alto Princeton

When rain falls hard
and cold winds blow,
where does everybody go?

Do you know?

3

When rain falls hard
and cold winds blow,
where do birds go?

To their nests.

When rain falls hard
and cold winds blow,
where do rabbits go?

To their burrows.

When rain falls hard
and cold winds blow,
where do spiders go?

Under the leaves.

When rain falls hard
and cold winds blow,
where do squirrels go?

Into the trees.

12

When rain falls hard
and cold winds blow,
where do foxes go?

To their dens.

When rain falls hard
and cold winds blow,
where do *you* go?